ANCIENT ADVENTURERS

A Collection of Essays

BY

SAMUEL MERRIFIELD BEMISS

EDITED BY

ANNIE LASH JESTER

WITH AN INTRODUCTION BY

JOHN MELVILLE JENNINGS

GARRETT & MASSIE • RICHMOND, VIRGINIA

1964

Second Printing, 1964

Library of Congress Catalog Number 59-14679
GARRETT & MASSIE, *Printers,* RICHMOND, VIRGINIA

TO
MARTHA WOODROOF HIDEN
1884 - 1959

Author's Note

This little book was written after careful basic research. Documentation of these articles was deposited with the Virginia Historical Society and may be examined there by students desiring to do so.

S.M.B.

INTRODUCTION

This volume of explorations into the early history of colonial Virginia is appropriately dedicated to the memory of Martha Woodroof Hiden. The author, Mr. Bemiss, had the good fortune to be associated with Mrs. Hiden in many of the cultural enterprises that occupied her time and, more particularly, served with her on the governing boards of the Virginia State Library, the Jamestown Corporation, and the Virginia Historical Society. His natural interest in the history of Virginia was stimulated by this association with a gentlewoman who lived and breathed the subject.

She was a great believer in first things first and consequently emphasized the need for collecting, preserving, and studying the materials that might shed light on the seventeenth century history of the state. This conviction, shared by Mr. Bemiss, established a bond between the two that was manifested in many beneficent conspiracies to promote historical research and activity. Mrs. Hiden's insistence that the wellsprings of colonial history had barely been tapped struck responsive chords in the mind of her colleague, for he secretly cherished a theory that the Virginian venture flowed from the convivial Elizabethan setting of the Mermaid Tavern.

Mrs. Hiden prevailed upon Mr. Bemiss on several occasions, especially while he was serving as president of the Virginia Historical Society, to address historical and patriotic organizations in which she was interested. Before the speaker knew what had happened, he was thrust from the part of patron into a role of active historical research and authorship. Indeed, Mrs. Hiden's enthusiasm for Virginia history encouraged many of her associates and friends to undertake projects which they would never have dreamed themselves capable of performing and which, but for her zeal and support, might initially have languished and failed.

This does not imply that Mrs. Hiden merely stood in the background spurring others to engage in productive historical pursuits. She herself, over a period of thirty years, was the author of innumerable scholarly contributions to the pages of the *Virginia Magazine of History and Biography*, the *William and Mary Quarterly, Second Series*, and *Tyler's Quarterly Historical and Genealogical Magazine*. She was co-author of *Newport News During the Second World War* (1948) and the invaluable *Adventurers of Purse and Person* (1956). One of the volumes in the Jamestown Historical Booklet series, *How Justice Grew* (1957), was the product of her pen, and had it not been for her characteristic determination the *Albemarle Parish (Surry and Sussex) Register* (1958) would never have appeared in print.

But Mrs. Hiden's unique contribution to Virginia historical research stemmed from her prodigious interest in the preservation of the local records of the state. For twenty-five years, at her own expense, she traveled back and forth between the county courthouses and the State Library in Richmond transporting, in all, over five hundred volumes of seventeenth and eighteenth century local records that were in desperate need of restoration. Every patriotic and local historical organization in Virginia felt the force of her determination to prosecute the program, for she was tireless in soliciting from them the funds needed for the actual restoration of the volumes.

This, of course, was only one of the useful services to scholarship which she performed in her quiet and modest way. None but her closest associates ever realized how much time, energy, and competence this seemingly frail lady expended in benefiting the fundamentals of Virginia historical research. In tribute to this life of useful service and in gratitude for generous personal encouragement, Mr. Bemiss has collected and printed in the present volume the essays and addresses that derive from the rewarding interest which he shared with Mrs. Hiden. He was assisted, appropriately enough, by another of Mrs. Hiden's associates and friends, Mrs. Lewis T. Jester, who edited the texts and, as Mrs. Hiden in her lifetime would probably have done, made a few minor corrections in the fresh and lively expositions that follow.

JOHN MELVILLE JENNINGS

Richmond, Virginia
June 4, 1959

CONTENTS

I.

THE JESUIT MISSION

SOME forty years or more before our famous little ships, the *Susan Constant*, the *Godspeed*, and the *Discovery*, brought Captain Newport and the English settlers to Virginia, a ship of the fleet of General Pedro Menendez, bearing Spanish adventurers, sailed into a beautiful bay which, in astonished admiration, they called "The Bay of the Mother of God."

Somewhere along the Virginia Peninsula, possibly in the great river which now bears the name of an English king, they were greeted by friendly and inquisitive Indians paddling canoes laden with furs and native products, which were traded for the white man's baubles.

Somehow, by persuasion or strong-arm methods, the Spaniards took away with them—to Havana, to Mexico, and later to Spain—a likely looking young Indian whom they educated in their best schools, baptized in their religion, and in honor of their viceroy in Mexico, gave to him the name of Don Luis de Valesco.

The identity of Don Luis is not known. Romance and conflicting accounts have obscured the records. He was described as an Indian prince, the son of a chieftain dwelling in a locality known as Ajacan. Having proved an apt pupil, he grew in favor with foster brothers and became the subject of considerable interest among the Spanish people. Welcomed in Spain as a prince by Philip II, he lived as a grandee, supported by a pension befitting his station. In America, he acted as an interpreter and an adviser in Indian affairs for General Menendez, and apparently was with him in the founding of Saint Augustine.

It was General Menendez who suggested to Philip that Don Luis be sent back to his native land of Ajacan to establish a permanent settle-

1

ment and claim that portion of the North American continent for Spain. Thus, on the expanding chessboard of Old World ambitions, pawns were made for desperate moves in the New. Somehow, to the north, France must be contained, and, likewise, the impudently intrepid followers of England's Virgin Queen.

The expedition was organized under the direction of General Menendez, and led by Father Segura, a man of unusual intellectual capabilities, devotion, and courage. It is worth noting that this expedition differed from other Spanish colonial attempts. Its leaders declining military protection, refused to be accompanied by soldiers. In the minds of the Jesuit fathers the mission's prime purpose was the conversion of the Indians.

The mission entered Chesapeake Bay in the autumn of 1570, celebrated mass in the locality of the modern shipyard at Newport News, and apparently guided by Don Luis, sailed up the James and at the mouth of College Creek just below Jamestown Island, landed nine Jesuit missionaries, including a youth, Alonzo de Olmos. Still guided by Don Luis, the missionaries made their way up College Creek, passed over the land now occupied by the City of Williamsburg, and proceeded down Queen's Creek to a point adjacent to the York River. Here, with the assistance of Don Luis, they built a house and set up their mission. The call of the wild was too much for Don Luis. The moral code of the Jesuits and that of the native Virginians differed to a marked degree. Apparently, the priests objected to some of the extracurricular activities of Don Luis, and so one morning Don Luis and friends borrowed a few axes from the missionaries and promptly hit them one and all, in the head. The boy Alonzo alone escaped to some friendly Indians in the neighborhood of Hampton where he was rescued by a relief ship in 1572. The relieving Spaniards satisfied their vengeance by hanging a few innocent Indians from the yardarms, and sailed away for Cuba. So ended the Spanish attempt to establish a settlement in Virginia.

The foregoing narrative is based on facts which were discovered in painstaking research by Father C. M. Lewis and Father A. J. Loomie, and made available to the Virginia Historical Society for publication. The documents which they reviewed and studied are original accounts by participants and eyewitnesses of the events, now preserved in the archives in Spain, in Cuba, and in Mexico. The translations from the original Latin and Spanish were made by competent scholars.

From these available records, representatives of the Virginia Historical Society, with Fathers Lewis and Loomie and Dr. Earl Gregg Swem, traced the course of the Spanish missionary ship from the Chesapeake Bay to College Creek.

The story is an integral part of the history of our Western World. The discovery of the manuscripts and the compilation of the records by Fathers Lewis and Loomie and Dr. Swem leave us forever indebted to these scholars.

II.

SIR WALTER RALEIGH

ALTHOUGH the extent of the influence exerted by the gentlemen of London's Mermaid Tavern on the development of the social and political institutions of the American people is not a matter of record, existence of that influence cannot be ignored. Nor, in larger measure, should the intrusion of these Englishmen in the events of the unfolding American drama be overlooked. According to tradition, Sir Walter Raleigh with his brilliant young friend Christopher Marlowe founded the most famous of all gentlemen's clubs. In the sixteenth century tavern gathered from time to time in stimulating, informal association most of England's great minds of the era, and here were discussed and possibly planned some of the outstanding events of the Elizabethan period. If it has been true in recent years that England's battles have been won on the playing fields of Harrow, it could be equally true that at the Mermaid the Armada was defeated, the great empire of Philip was shaken to its foundation, the North American continent was wrested from Spain, and that here Shakespeare found the types for some of the characters in his plays.

Stimulated in thought, men of the period vied to outstrip their fellows in the deeds conceived. The Queen called the plays and made the rules. She was quick to recognize ability and needed the possessors of it. She needed gold, and her henchmen found it moral and convenient to take it on the high seas. To supplement her income Hawkins found it harmonious with Christian ethics to raid the African coast for Negroes. The Queen formed joint stock companies with her subjects and advanced funds to her favorites, Raleigh in particular, to finance adventures, which in another period would be termed piracy.

5

Shakespeare certainly had before him at the Mermaid the very counterparts for characters he sought to create. Although he may have attempted to satirize Raleigh and his particular group in one of his poorer plays, he endowed the famous Hamlet with "the noble mind" and presented him as a courtier, soldier and scholar, all which designations fit Sir Walter, although the Queen's favorite was never afflicted with Hamlet's indecision. Also, there are evidences of the character of that militant divine Richard Hakluyt, possibly of Hawkins and the sea captain Grenville; and when the playwright described the men "whose minds were tossing on the ocean where their rich argosies with portly sail did o'er peer the petty traffickers," he may have had in mind the Smiths and the Sandys. Bacon did have a library which he "valued above a dukedom," and in a Mortimer or a Percy there may be glimpses of an Essex or a Leicester. These were among the men who planned and discussed adventures at the Mermaid. It would almost appear that the subscription list to the Virginia Company had been passed around among them and that the composition of Christopher Newport's company had been a subject of discussion, or that Bacon's "Essay on Plantations" had been based on Newport's experience.

The man credited with founding the circle of brilliant minds assembling informally at the Mermaid, was also the man, who, above all others, gave direction to the destiny of Virginia. As a star in the unfolding drama of England's greatest era, he crossed the stage many times. In courage, liberalism, industry and energy, the leaders of the first colonists were akin to him. From him they received the vision which fired their deeds and sustained them through hardship.

Sir Walter was indeed the soldier, the courtier, the scholar, but more he was a scientist, a philosopher, an historian, a naval strategist, the greatest contemporary naval architect, a first class pirate, a poet, and with all a gentle lover. As Captain of the Guard at Elizabeth's court he was the Queen's bodyguard, and chief henchman. As a singer of songs and writer of delicate verse, he played on the heart strings of the Virgin Queen. He could write on a window pane where she would be sure to see it:

> "Fain would I climb, but fear I to fall;"

and with wit and hope she could challenge:

> "If thy heart fail thee, climb not at all."

He could wage relentless war against the Irish, sack Cadiz, prepare a squadron to raid the plate fleet, participate in a brawl, and pray:

"Give me my scollop shell of quiet,
My staff of faith to walk upon,
My scrip of joy, immortal diet,
My bottle of salvation,
My gown of glory, hope's true gage!
And thus I'll make my pilgrimage."

He was banished from court for falling in love with the Queen's lady in waiting, the beauteous Elizabeth Throckmorton. Notwithstanding, he remained steadfast to her throughout a long and beautiful romance to the end of his day. She preserved his head in a red leather bag to her death. Afterwards, Bishop Goodman testified, "I know where his skull is kept to this day, and I have kissed it."

He was sent to the Tower on false charges by a stupid king who was afraid of him, but prison could not suppress his great energy or activity. During his confinement he wrote his *History of the World* which was acclaimed by the world. He participated in establishing the Bodleian Library. He conducted botanical and pharmaceutical experiments and produced an elixir from an Indian bark, which in all probability was the introduction of quinine to our medicine. But these were just footprints on the path trod by the great man and facets in his life which reflected the light from the firmament under which he moved. His life was England—restless, legendary and vital, heedless of ethics and ruthless, dominated by twin passions, which were to keep out that desolation which masqueraded on the continent under the cloak of religion and were to reduce the power of Spain. English piracy, the answer to Spanish bigotry, was part of the program. To quote a contemporary historian, it was Elizabeth's "constant practice to annoy the Spaniard through those mighty sonnes of Neptune, Drake, Raleigh, Frobisher and Cavendish." The galleons and carracks they captured enriched the land, stimulated adventure and laid the groundwork for colonizing America.

Raleigh was born in 1552. At fourteen he entered Oxford. Two years later he was in France fighting for the Huguenots. In 1580, as a captain of infantry, he followed the Gilberts and other Devon relatives to Ireland to suppress the rebellion of the Earl of Desmond. His ruthlessness and bravery became traditional with both friend and foe.

In an appearance before the Privy Council in 1581, his quick wit, decision and imperious manner attracted the Queen's interest. She loved a soldier, and she loved this one too well to want him to go back to Ireland "to get knocked on the head." And, so, his rise to fortune and power became impressive; he was a bright star, envied by both the greater and lesser lights who continually sought his eclipse.

Raleigh received his letters patent in March, 1584, "to discover and to plant Christian inhabitants in places convenient upon those large and ample countries extended northward from the cape of Florida, not in the actual possession of any Christian prince." From this date and by this patent the destiny of the North American continent was determined. He was responsible for the exploratory expedition which named this vast territory Virginia, and found "the main to be the goodliest soil under the cope of Heaven."

The language of this patent is significant. The French to the far north were interested in the rich fur trade, the Spaniards to the far south were enslaving the Indians and destroying ancient civilizations for the gold and the precious stones which the operation yielded. The Englishman was interested in real estate because of the opportunity it offered for productive effort and the right of the individual to enjoy the fruits of his labor; and Raleigh the scientist, the botanist, the agriculturalist, was interested in what the land could produce with the application of intelligent labor. He experimented with all sorts of plants and trees. He experimented with industry and labor. In the New World the Englishman's home was to become his castle.

But Good Queen Bess died, and he whom a brother monarch termed "the wisest fool in Christendom" came to the throne. He feared Sir Walter, the ablest and most versatile man of his age. He feared him because of his liberalism which the King called atheism, for his patriotism which he termed disloyalty, for his ability which was universally recognized, and for his courage which was unlimited. Robert Cecil had said of Raleigh, "I know he can toil terribly."

And, so, on false charges Jamie the Scot, in personal fear, bent the pregnant hinges of the knee to Philip, tried Raleigh by a court in the pay of the Spaniard, and "put him to death chiefly for giving them satisfaction," as James himself pleaded. But Sir Walter was old, he was sixty-five, he had "toiled terribly," his great work was done. He had lived with life and death as equals. More than any other man, he had laid the cornerstone of America. On the night before he went to the scaffold he wrote:

> "Even such is time! who takes in trust
> Our youth, our joys and all we have,
> And pays us but with earth and dust
> Who in the dark and silent grave,
> When we have wandered all our ways,
> Shuts up the story of our days.
> But from that earth, that grave, that dust,
> My God shall raise me up, I trust."

Sir Walter's story is not shut up and his God has raised up the man whose spirit and work still live in Virginia, the man who took as his motto early in life, *Nec mortem peto, nec finem fugio.*

III.
CHRISTOPHER NEWPORT, MARINER

IN the England of Elizabeth men lived dangerously. It was the way of life. The fearless Queen, living in the midst of many who sought her destruction, set a superb standard of personal courage and self-mastery, which was contagious. It marked the character of her captains, the incomparable guardians of her person and her kingdom. Bright stars, whose exploits at any other time would have earned a place among those of Britain's immortals, moved in her brilliant firmament, unacclaimed and almost unnoticed. In our day, historians are searching ancient records in an attempt to appraise the influence and measure the magnitude of those lesser lights, and of the events in which they participated. Biographical sketches must be pieced together with material from many sources, for Elizabeth's actors scarcely realized that they were the makers of history.

In some ways Christopher Newport seems quite un-Elizabethan. This mariner who, in his maturity, was to be known as the Admiral of Virginia was a commander without guile. He was courteous to his enemies, loyal to his superiors, and his justice was tempered with humanity. He was not avaricious. Nothing is known of his ancestry or his education. As a youth he went to sea, probably in his early teens. The careers of Gilbert, Hawkins, Drake, Raleigh, Frobisher and others appealed to his imagination. By sea lay the path to renown. On the seas moved the wealth of nations.

In an admiralty case involving the division of spoils from a privateering adventure, Newport testified on November 23, 1590, that he was ". . . thirty years of age or thereabouts." At that time his reputation as a successful and enterprising gentleman pirate was estab-

11

lished and his services much sought after in England's Merchant Navy —that illusive and uncoordinated power, the acts of which the Queen could disclaim responsibility, but through which the life blood of England flowed. Daring men and nimble ships in the service of English merchants, sometimes engaged in honest trade, generally in privateering, shared Raleigh's avowed purpose "to singe the beard of the King of Spain wherever he could be found." Their successful adventures laid the foundation for England's empire. The Queen, for foreign consumption, might appear to be outdone by the exploits of Raleigh or Drake and their agents, and threaten to send them to the Tower but when her share of the loot was delivered she knighted her bad boys. Under righteous pressure she could remonstrate with Hawkins for his activities in the African slave trade with his ships the *Jesus* and the *John the Baptist*, but when he explained that he was lifting the Negro to salvation through servitude she accepted her share of the profits.

Raleigh called her the "Shepherdess of the Seas." Philip II called her the "Queen of Pirates." History has accorded her both honors.

Newport is first positively identified with the English merchant fleet in admiralty papers concerning the cruise of the *Minion*. This ship under the command of Stephen Hare sailed from London in 1580 to trade with the Portuguese colony in Brazil. Trouble developed between the master and his crew. At Bahia, fearing the wrath of Hare, Newport and a companion, Abraham Cocke, went ashore and were left when the *Minion*, attacked by a Portuguese ship, sailed away. Cocke remained in Brazil for seven years, but Newport, by means unknown, made his way back to England, for, in the year 1587, he appears to have been a mariner of authority in the forces under Drake in the fantastic destruction of the Spanish fleet in the harbor of Cadiz. That he shared Drake's confidence is revealed in testimony of the affair published by the Navy Records Society; that he conducted himself with credit is certain, for, later in the same year, as master's mate, he was aboard the *Drake*, a ship owned by John Watts, merchant prince of privateers, cruising off the coast of Spain seeking prizes and other opportunities to damage the prestige of the mighty Catholic King.

The thoroughness with which the master minds of English strategy, Drake, Howard, and Raleigh, organized their forces to defeat the Armada in 1588, certified that every competent mariner had a definite assignment in that naval epic. There were three participating ships named *Drake*. Which Newport was on is uncertain, but that he served on one cannot be doubted.

Newport's reputation as a trustworthy associate and an able, God-fearing pirate waxed as his exploits multiplied. His advancement was rapid for, by 1589, he appeared as Master of the *Margaret* on a privateering adventure financed by three famous London merchants—Cobb, Moore and Southwick. The extent of the financial success of this cruise is not clear, but several prizes were taken and the plunder disposed of for enough to reward the crew of the *Margaret* for their pains, to pay the Lord High Admiral his statutory share, and to reward the syndicate for its risk. This cruise of the *Margaret* completed the young Captain's preparation for further responsibilities and greater adventures. In 1590, at the age of thirty, he was given his first command and with it began his service in and to the western world.

Early in 1590, William Sanderson, Raleigh's chief supporter in his overseas adventures—for the twofold purpose of visiting Raleigh's Roanoke Colony and seeking prizes in the Caribbean—secured the release of three ships belonging to the London merchant, John Watts. The ships were the *Hopewell* under Captain Abraham Cocke, Newport's companion in the *Minion* mutiny in 1580, the *John Evangelist* under Captain Wm. Lane, and the *Little John* under Newport. The little fleet left Plymouth March 20, setting its course and timing its departure to intercept the treasure ships from the Spanish Main, which customarily assembled in some West Indian port before sailing under convoy for Spain. Invariably, the treasure fleet scheduled its movements and rendezvous in an effort to clear the Caribbean and South Atlantic before the hurricane season. Therefore, the months of June and July provided the most exciting hunting for the English privateer.

Newport's little fleet arrived at Dominica, a Windward Island, early in May. Plans for operation were simple. The ships separated, cruising along the known lanes of Spanish shipping in search of prizes, reassembling at appointed places at frequent intervals and generally maintaining some sort of contact with one another. Suitable prizes captured were manned and added to the fleet or, if the situation warranted, loaded with loot and sent to a friendly port. Thus, they cruised the waters between Hispaniola and the neighboring islands until

July 2, somewhat discouraged and fearing that the plate fleet had passed them by.

On that date Newport's fleet was joined by Sanderson's ship, the *Moonlight*, under Captain Spicer, and her consort a pinnace of thirty tons under Captain Harris. Almost at the same time the Spanish treasure fleet of fourteen ships appeared on the horizon. Immediately the English sailed in pursuit forcing the Spanish to scatter. Before nightfall Newport in the *Little John* had taken a prize. In the early hours of the next morning the *Hopewell* and the *Moonlight*, by chance, found themselves alongside the great ship *El Buen Jesus*, Vice-Admiral of the Spanish fleet. A brisk encounter ended in the capture of the richest prize of the venture. A prize crew was placed aboard under Captain Hallet and *El Buen Jesus* with all her riches departed for the Azores and England where she arrived safely to the substantial enrichment of the London merchants. While the fight with the *Jesus* was in progress Newport on the *Little John* and Lane on the *Evangelist* overtook the main Spanish squadron, desperately trying to make port in Jamaica. Details of the ensuing fight are not available. Spanish documents reveal its intensity. Only half the fleet, much damaged, reached harbor. The rest were taken as prizes or sunk after cargoes had been salvaged.

The summer was now well advanced. The hurricane season was approaching. So, after several days rest, Newport freed his prisoners and set his sail for the Bahama Channel, hoping to join the rest of his fleet with their prizes and a triumphant return home. Rounding the western tip of Cuba about nightfall he sighted three Spanish ships of the Mexican fleet. One escaped during the night. At daylight Newport attacked the other two. Furious and bloody was the fight. Newport had his right arm "strooken off" and his lieutenant was killed. One Spanish ship was sunk, the other boarded. Part of her cargo was transferred to the *Little John*, but then, seeing other Spanish ships coming to help the stricken ship, Newport gave up the fight and headed out to sea. He arrived at Portsmouth September 19 and thus ended his first adventurous voyage to the West Indies. The *Hopewell*, the *Evangelist* and the *Moonlight* with their prizes got safely back to England. The *Hopewell* had visited Roanoke Island to find only the word "Croatan" carved on a tree. The twofold mission had been fulfilled.

To Newport this voyage was not altogether a success. He had lost his arm. Much of the booty he had captured was lost in sunken ships. His own financial harvest is uncertain. Yet, for England he had struck a telling blow. Spanish treasure laden galleons and frigates would not again sail the western seas with impunity. With his crew and the merchants he had earned esteem for dependability, loyalty, and intrepid courage. His reputation was established, and henceforth his services were always in demand. The effect on Spain was a little less than appalling. Spanish dignitaries and ministers attested to this. Juan de Oribe Apallua wrote from Havana to the Crown in September 1590, "They have chased or seized every vessel entering or leaving this harbor." Juan de Texeda wrote, "These audacious Englishmen, without shame dared them at their very doors." In fact, the privateersmen had caused consternation and amazement in every Caribbean port.

Fragmentary accounts of Newport's activities during the autumn of 1590 may be gathered from documents in English archives. He appeared before the Admiralty Court to substantiate his claim to prizes and cargoes taken during the summer. His mind was active with maturing plans for the next summer while his wounds were attended. English merchant adventurers were eager for his services.

Early in 1591, before the good hunting season started in the Caribbean, as Captain of the *Margaret* owned by Robert Cobb of London, with the *Prudence* in consort under Captain John Brough, he set out ostensibly on a trading expedition to the Mediterranean and the West Coast of Africa, but his real purpose was to annoy the King of Spain and glean as much wealth as he could in the enterprise. Whatever trading was done in Africa was certainly incidental, for soon dispatches from every port in the West Indies announced the awe-inspiring presence of the one-armed Englishman who struck with the suddenness of a tropical storm, sank ships, confiscated goods, and treated his prisoners with kindness.

The Spanish had written that the English were good sailors but better pirates. That they were good sailors is attested by their exploits. That they were better pirates is attested by the wealth they brought home, which aided London on her way to a position as the banking capital of the world. The Queen's enterprising mariners had found Spain's most vulnerable spot, her source of indispensable wealth which could be protected only at the cost of leaving home ports unguarded.

This was Philip's dilemma which the English exploited with all their vigor. Summer trips to the Caribbean became annual affairs for the English adventurers.

Newport's cruise in 1592 proved to be the most significant in his privateering career. Financed by his former backers Robert Cobb and veteran associates, he sailed from Dover in February in command of a well-equipped fleet of four vessels. His ship, which he made famous, was the *Golden Dragon*, a name amply justified by the audacity of her Captain and the harvest she returned to England. The other ships were the *Prudence,* the *Margaret,* and the *Virginia*. The fleet arrived in the West Indies early in April where for a few days the men refreshed themselves "a fishing and a fowling" and bathing in the warm springs of the Islands. The general alarm which spread rapidly through the Islands both helped and hindered their purposes. Inhabitants of coastal towns abandoned their homes and took their wealth to the hills. Shipping sought refuge in protected harbors, into which the intrepid English sailed at will destroying defending galleys and taking whatever met their fancy.

At Puerto de Cavallos, to deceive its defenders, they hoisted the Spanish flag and captured a warship almost in the shadow of the castle. In that town they found six tons of quicksilver, sixteen tuns of old sack, and despoiled the Catholic Church but did not burn the two hundred houses, for, as Corporal John Twitt of the *Golden Dragon* wrote, "We found other contentment,—and having taken our pleasure sailed back again for Truxillo." Hakluyt published Twitt's good account of the voyage which also relates that, "We took and burnt upon the coast of Hispaniola, and within the Bay of Honduras three towns, and nineteen sail of ships and frigates." As successes multiplied and the season advanced, captured ships were dispatched for home port with plunder. Fortune had thus far smiled on the bold enterprise. As the time approached for the fleet to turn homeward a severe storm struck scattering the ships. Those that survived the storm sought their separate ways to England. Off the coast of Florida, Newport alone with his consort the *Prudence* took another prize laden with tobacco. He visited friendly Indians for several days, repaired and watered his ships and then set his course for the Azores.

The *Golden Dragon* and the *Prudence* arrived at Flores on July 26 and there Newport joined Sir John Burgh, Captain of the famous

Roebuck commanding Raleigh's privateering fleet. A formal consortship was drawn up to cover their cooperative activities including command of the fleet and division of spoils. The agreement covered the period from July 28 to September 10. As senior officer Sir John took command of the combined fleet consisting in all of seven ships which he spread out west of the Azores hoping to intercept the Spanish carracks, returning from the East Indies.

On August 3rd, "the *Dainty* had first sight of the huge carrack, *Madre de Dios*. Being of excellent sail she got the start of the rest of the fleet and fetched up with her between eleven and twelve o'clock in the morning." And so, the account of an eyewitness continues: "the *Dainty* and the *Dragon* were the first that came up to her and finding her no less than a carrack might not offer any meaner courtesy than to hail her with a cannon, but she being not unmindful bestowed the like on them, for she made small account of our ships." At this juncture Newport addressed his men: " 'Masters now the time is come that either we must end our days or take yon carrick'. He wished his company to stand to their charge like men and if any displeasure were among them to forget and forgive. Then the Master of the *Golden Dragon* took a cup of wine and drank to John Locke, the master's mate, and so throughout the ship every one drank to the other."

A bloody and furious fight, well documented in British Admiralty reports, lasted until two o'clock next morning; then, the small English ships overcame the mighty floating fortress, the greatest single prize which had ever been taken on the high seas. To Newport, Sir John Burgh accorded the high honor as well as the responsibility of taking the great *Madre de Dios* to Dartmouth. Even after she had been thoroughly looted by the sailors who adorned the barmaids of Devon with silks and jewels there remained enough for Raleigh to realize £24,000, Cumberland £37,000, the London merchants £12,000 and the Queen £90,000. Newport's rewards enabled him to buy a garden and comfortable home on Tower Hill in London. Here he maintained his family for the rest of his life. The mighty carrack eventually rotted away in Dartmouth harbor.

As the older great captains serving in England's navies passed on their places were taken by younger men of equal sagacity, courage, and energy. It was they who finished the task begun by Hawkins, Frobisher, Grenville, and Drake; it was they who cleared the seas of the enemy and prepared the way for the permanent settlement of Virginia. The success of the 1592 expeditions inspired the merchants to greater ventures and the mariners to exceeding boldness. In 1593 Newport on the *Golden Dragon* with Sir John Burgh on the *Roebuck* was out again. Sir William Munson noted in his Naval Tract that they returned with success, which always meant sunken ships and despoiled Spanish towns in the West Indies.

In 1594, still financed by the Cobb-Moore syndicate, he was out again on the *Golden Dragon,* sinking Spanish ships and gathering plunder; and, so, to the end of the aging Queen's reign, his well organized and ably directed expeditions continued to terrorize the Caribbean.

In 1596 Newport became part owner of the *Neptune* with the prominent goldsmiths Francis and Richard Glanvill. These gentlemen were established bankers in their age and were, therefore, primarily interested in gold, silver, and precious stones. The dependable Newport conducted himself accordingly. The bulky cargoes captured were sold for cash, the towns were ransomed. In 1599, at Travasco, he acquired "888 ounces of plate, £200 in Spanish coin, 41 ounces of pearls and gold, and went home with the bells of the town."

The cruise of 1602 is shrouded in mystery but John Chamberlayne wrote to Dudley Carlton that, "Newport with two other ships hath taken 5 frigates laden with treasure coming from Cartagena—if all be true that is reported, it will prove the greatest prize that ever I heard of—two millions at least. The King of Spain hath sent out eight men of war to waylay him." But Newport was never successfully waylaid.

The Queen died in 1603. Her timid successor made peace, ending the war which had lasted sixteen years. The great team of merchants and mariners with the blessings of the Crown had completed their assignment. With the Royal Navy they had cleared the seas of enemies and curbed the power of the King of Spain. The treaty, as it was officially proclaimed, "was the means under God of making possible the settlement of English colonies across the Atlantic battleground, in the far distant land of Virginia." And, so, that peace ended the privateering career of Christopher Newport, "the foremost mariner of his time." The wealth he had brought home provided an effective stimulant to the business of the London merchants. It provided capital and goods for transition from war to peace and it lent vigor to a developing society of bankers and storekeepers. Newport's employment had always been with the London merchants. It was to continue so to the end of his life.

During the succeeding two years after the long war ended Newport made two more trips to his old familiar battlegrounds but in pursuit of peaceful trade, and doubtless also to learn whatever he could concerning Spanish intentions for colonial expansion north of Florida.

He was as familiar as any man with the Atlantic seaboard; it is even probable that he had visited the Chesapeake area. In any event his experience and ability caused Sir Thomas Smith, the Grocers, the Salters, the Skinners, and the whole association of merchants in the London Company to select him to organize and transport 105 carefully selected Englishmen to the land of Virginia to establish there England's claim to a portion of the New World. Between 1607 and his last voyage in 1611, on which he brought Sir Thomas Dale, he made five trips to the little fort and village which he had founded, and which was named Jamestown in honor of his King. Twice he directed the building of the fort and twice he saw to the building of the church. Twice he saved John Smith from hanging, and many times he quieted dissensions so ardent that the colony's existence was threatened. Under his supervision, his crew built the *Patience* and the *Deliverance* from native cedar to rescue the shipwrecked colonists at Bermuda. On each trip to Virginia he brought fresh courage, men, supplies and the news. He brought the first women to make homes at Glass House Point; he saw established America's first manufacturing industry. He provided that indispensable link with England which gave her colony its permanence. He was the first English explorer of the rivers on both sides of the Virginia Peninsula, and under his direction Tindall made the first maps of the area, one of which is still extant.

In 1612 he was appointed one of the six masters of the Royal Navy and assigned the responsibility of taking Sir Robert Shirley to Persia as England's Ambassador. In 1614 he was made an Admiral of the East India Company and given the honor of taking Sir Thomas Rice as England's first Ambassador to the Court of the Grand Mogul.

An old report to the London Company contains a sentence which characterizes the mariner's brilliant career: "Newport performed his duties as charged." What more could one add? "All that which should accompany old age,—honor, obedience, troops of friends" crowned his days. When home from the sea he lived on Tower Hill with his wife, two sons and two daughters, master of a comfortable house and garden. One son followed the maritime calling of his father and served with him. As master's mate young Christopher was aboard the *Hope* in 1617 when his father "sunk to rest in the far off waters of India." Newport died as he had lived—on the sea—and the sea received his honored body draped in his Country's flag as the ship of which he was Captain bowed in reverence with the movement of the wind and the waves.

Newport's memorial in this country is Newport News. There in the spring of 1607 he established a "store", and stationed a few men to guard the entrance of the river. It is fitting that at that same location are built the ships which guard this great nation today.

IV.

THE THREE SHIPS

ON December 20, 1606, an event far reaching in consequences occurred at Blackwall's wharf. On that day, three small ships with 105 adventurers aboard dropped down the Thames and began their voyage to Virginia. Those ships carried with them the genesis of a new nation and were ladened with the cornerstone to support it. The departure was the climactic outcome of years of careful planning. Moreover, it was a crucial play on the international chessboard of power politics in an arena of teriffic intensities, for the English settlement of North America became a sturdy link in a chain of events, resulting in the checkmate of the King of Spain and the eventual eclipse of his widespread power. The seeds the English colony planted in the goodly Virginia soil yielded abundantly, and upon the cornerstone the adventurers laid, rests the power of a mighty people.

The word adventurer did not then connote a reckless seeker after excitement and plunder, but rather a wise and courageous man who took a calculated risk that his labor and his capital might yield a profit. The Gilberts and Sir Humphrey's half-brother Sir Walter Raleigh, many years earlier, had conceived the idea of an English settlement in North America. The godmother of the enterprise, although deceased when it got under way, was certainly Queen Elizabeth, herself; for, as Thomas Fuller observed: "It was for her that God set up a generation of military men by land and sea, who were like a suit of clothes made for her and worn out by her." Sixteenth century English mariners had given the Virgin Queen a command upon the seas which led to Britain's eventual domination of all seven of the seas.

The first act of this world drama—the birth of a nation—had required great actors to prepare the scene. In the association of military men and mariners noted by Fuller there might readily have been included the great merchants, the philosophers, and the poets, for that was the generation of Thomas Smith and the Sandys, of Bacon and Hooker, and of Shakespeare, Marlowe and Johnson. The mariners, Drake, Cavendish, Grenville and Hawkins had opened the sea lanes and set a tempo of incomparable courage, endurance, and achievement. Men dedicated to purposeful adventure had superseded the ancient feudal nobility. The merchant princes and the goldsmiths had financed the ventures which added luster to the England of Elizabeth. That exacting mistress had said of her subjects: "Make them earn their honor and by pain and peril purchase what place of credit or profit is bestowed on them." And so, every man in that vibrant and dynamic society was required to justify his position.

Ample evidence substantiates the assumption of friendly intercourse among the gentlemen of the Elizabethan period. The press agent of English adventure, Richard Hakluyt, the minister, dedicated his *Voyages* to Raleigh; Sir Edward Coke, the Lord Chief Justice, necessarily had a hand in the first Charter of the Virginia Company; Sir Francis Bacon collaborated in drawing the second; the Earl of Southampton was a patron of the Company. Sir Richard Martin, three times Lord Mayor of London, had a son on the *Godspeed,* who had also sailed around the world with Drake, and commanded a ship in Grenville's fleet. The Earl of Northumberland had a brother on the *Susan Constant.* Sir Thomas Gates and Sir George Somers were enthusiastic backers of the venture. The subscription list to the shares in the Virginia Company had been passed around at the Globe and the Black Friars, and the undertaking was certainly discussed at those gentlemen's clubs, assembled at the Mermaid and the Miter. It is not possible that the author of *Hamlet* and *The Tempest* received only the plaudits of his fellow actors. In the stimulating association between thinkers and performers of a brilliant period action invariably became the complement of ideas.

To recreate that scene at Blackwall on that December day requires some imagination as there are few available records depicting the occasion of the departure for Virginia. Since the miracle of the development of the social and political fabric of America hardly would have occurred except for the prior informal association of the great liberal

Elizabethans, it is reasonable to conclude that some of them stood on the wharf as the little ships cast off their lines. They were a brave and impressive company waving farewells and breathing prayers to the God in whom they trusted that the adventurers would have a safe crossing. It is likely that the most versatile man of that age, imprisoned in the Tower by a stupid King, also watched those ships float down the river past the most famous of English ships, Drake's *Golden Hind,* while petty traffickers on that outgoing tide reverently signaled farewells. The tide of Raleigh's life now was at ebb, yet, at the same time, the departure of the three ships marked a climax for him—the fruit of his labor.

Not much is known about the three ships except their weight and dimensions. They were old ships, at least one of which was chartered for the voyage from the Muscovy Company. The names of two of them even were uncertain, an uncertainty erased by findings of the Virginia 350th Anniversary Commission, approved by the Virginia Assembly. Research established the ships as: the *Susan Constant,* one hundred tons, Captain Newport commanding; the *Godspeed,* forty tons, Captain Gosnold commanding; the *Discovery,* twenty tons, Captain Ratcliffe commanding.

These captains had been to America before as had members of their crews and their company. They were chosen for their experience, and they were competent mariners else they never could have brought those small vessels together across the Atlantic Ocean. Captain Newport had made many trips as a privateersman and a trader. Captain Gosnold had surveyed the New England coast in 1602, and built a fort on Elizabeth Island. He discovered and named Cape Cod. Captain Ratcliffe, listed in the Virginia Company records as Captain Sicklemore, alias Ratcliffe, whom John Smith had described as a poor, counterfeit impostor, had fought through the campaigns in the Low Country and his opinion of Smith was at least as contemptuous as Smith's opinion of him.

By way of contrast it is to be remembered that the *Mayflower* was a ship of 170 tons—almost twice as large as the *Susan Constant*—and that her passengers had fled from England to Holland and were fleeing from Holland to a great wilderness very much after the pattern of the flight of the Children of Israel from the wrath of Pharoah. Their prime objective was an independent theocratic, autocratic state the principles of behavior of which were the ordinances of the Hebrew Old Testament. They succeeded in establishing and maintaining such a state for seventy years.

The passengers on these three ships lifted their eyes to different horizons. They adventured their all that they might have life more abundant—spiritually, politically, materially. They opposed arbitrary government in any form. The two groups of Englishmen in their ideologies were poles apart in England and they were poles apart after they landed in Massachusetts and Virginia, as were other colonists. If one seeks to understand the miracle of America he must examine these contrasts—not only these, but the other elements thrown in the great crucible by the proprietaries of Carolina and Catholic Maryland, by the Quakers of Pennsylvania, the Dutch of New York, and the Rhode Islanders of Roger Williams. All were tested, and for 175 years were tempered on the anvil of our colonialism until the strong metal of our nationalism became fused in the provisions of our Bill of Rights and the articles of the Constitution of the United States.

Every expedition in that early day necessarily had a military complexion. The order of the Council was that "Captain Newport shall have sole charge and command of all captains, soldiers, mariners and other persons that shall go in any of the said ships." But this expedition had a practical aspect also. The adventurers were essentially builders. They brought with them seed for the soil and tools to build permanent homes—and, above all, a dream of empire. Space does not permit a further description of persons and characters. It suffices to say that in the group were ambitious gentlemen, worthy mariners, bricklayers, carpenters, a blacksmith, a tailor, a barber, a drummer, laborers and forty sailors.

Storms and contrary winds held the fleet in the Downs for six weeks. Finally the ships departed taking the southern route by the Azores and the West Indies. They cruised around the West Indies visiting various islands refreshing themselves in the clear waters of crystal springs. They enjoyed the tropical fruits, and on the Island of Nevis they remained six days "a fowling and a fishing." On the Island of Mona the first and only death during the voyage occurred, that of a gentleman, Edward Brooks, whose "fat melted within him in the great heat."

It is true that dissension had occurred among the company; possibly it was frequent. Dissension landed John Smith in chains, and, for the first time, while he was employed by the Virginia Company he was threatened with hanging. It is to be remembered that twice again during his two years in Virginia he was in similar danger before, as George Percy related, "He was finally sent to England with thirty unruly youths, none of whom were desired at Jamestown."

When one considers these ships one wonders at the completed miracle. The space between decks was so low that it was necessary to crawl into the living quarters, and the decks were incapable of holding the whole company even in fair weather. However, on April 26, about 4 o'clock in the morning, the lookouts descried the land of Virginia and the same day the ships entered the Bay of Chesapeake, ending the voyage of four months. After some judicious exploring they sailed up Powhatan's great river and moored their ships in six fathoms of water to the goodly tall trees which grew to the very water's edge. In thirty days they built a fort which has taken a year to reproduce with modern tools; but the story after their landing is another act in this drama. It is a story of hardships. At the same time it is a story of the recognition of the dignity of productive labor, and of the recognition of the right of free men to govern themselves, and, in all, it is the greatest of success stories.

The replicas of these ships are moored at Jamestown. They are symbols of our fathers' indomitable courage; they are symbols of our faith in the God who guides our destiny; they are symbols of man's aspiration and striving; they are symbols of our immortal American heritage.

V.
JOHN MARTIN

IN the first quarter of the seventeenth century Englishmen first committed themselves unreservedly to the soil of the vast western continent and planted in Virginia the genesis of a new nation. The great adventure was sponsored by practical men, the ablest businessmen of their era, who had bound themselves together in a joint-stock enterprise, the Virginia Company of London. Their aggressiveness in support of free enterprise and parliamentary government incurred the hostility of James I and his Stuart successors, resulting in the revocation of the Company's charter and the destruction or impounding of its records. Our early historians who dealt with this period, John Smith, Robert Beverley, William Stith, and the great letter writers were sympathetic to the feudal prerogatives of the King or were deliberately attempting to attract royal favor.

The story of Jamestown may be crystallized in the life of one of the actors in the great drama. John Martin landed at Jamestown with Christopher Newport in the spring of 1607, outlived others of the original company, and probably died at Brandon his estate on the James about 1632.

A knowledge of the English background of the ancient adventurers is essential to any understanding of the miracle they achieved. Martin's life was in many respects typical of those who played major roles. Courage, energy, and determination were essential qualities of colonists who survived and succeeded in establishing homes and a new way of life in the New World. Born about 1562, the third son of Richard Martin, a London goldsmith, John was a junior member of that generation of men who achieved for England's Virgin Queen

control on the seas, and gave military and literary brilliance to the
Elizabethan era. In the great events of those days he played his part—
contentious, selfish, perhaps ruthless when occasion demanded, but
courageous, energetic, and determined. These qualities guaranteed
the success of the Virginia colony.

That John Martin had visited America before he came to Jamestown
with Christopher Newport cannot be questioned. Richard Martin had
been one of the chief backers of Sir Francis Drake on his voyage
around the world, and the John Martin who accompanied the Admiral
was almost certainly the young son of the goldsmith. *The World
Encompassed* does not mention him by name, but tells of his experiences, his wounds in combat, and his association with Sir Francis.
He is identified by Francis Fletcher, chaplain of the expedition, in his
account of the voyage. Martin was privy to the enterprises, the dreams,
and the rewards of that great expedition and undoubtedly was enriched by a share of the loot brought home in the *Golden Hind.*

Later he had sailed with Drake as captain of the *Benjamin,* 140
tons or less, into Vigo Bay "chiefly for the purpose of insulting the
King of Spain in one of his home ports." He had sailed on with the
Admiral to sack Spanish settlements in the Cape Verde Islands, in
the Caribbean, St. Augustine, and had relieved Lane and Raleigh's
colony at Roanoke Island, transporting the survivors back to England.
He was a skilled mariner and accustomed to command. He had earned
his rank as captain in the Queen's Navy. No record of his having
served against the Spanish Armada has been discovered, but it is not
probable that this follower of Drake, who characteristically participated
in every available brawl, missed the opportunity to participate in the
greatest of Elizabethan England's naval exploits.

Richard Martin, the father, had come to London as a young man
from Saffron, Walden, Essex County, apprenticed himself to a goldsmith, and mastered the trade. In 1558 we find him in partnership
with Hugh Kagle at the Sign of the Harp, Goldsmith's Row—bankers
and goldsmiths to her Majesty—and married to Dorcas, the daughter
of Sir John Eggleston of Lancashire. That was an age when the
merchant, the banker, and the successful businessman eclipsed and
supplanted the ancient nobility and captured man's imagination by
their expanding activities, the work of their hands, and the specula-
tions of their minds. Richard Martin grew in importance and in royal

favor. He served successively as warden and master of the mint, as alderman, and thrice as Lord Mayor of London, and was knighted. He, with Sir Thomas Gresham and Sir Martin Bowes, formed that trio of great banker statesmen of Elizabeth's England who pointed the way to their successors who eventually made London the banking capital of the world. Sir Richard's son John married Mary, daughter of Robert Brandon, goldsmith of London, and his daughter Dorcas, married Sir Julius Caesar, Master of the Rolls and intimate of Francis Bacon. John Martin ever turned to Sir Julius, his brother-in-law and friend, when he was in trouble. Incidentally, there are woods at Brandon still known as "Caesar's Woods."

Sir Richard's stature as a great man grew, but he was embarrassed by the debts due him by courtiers and the Queen herself. He died insolvent at about the age of eighty-six. Sir Francis Bacon interceded with the government in behalf of his widow.

In 1589 a list of debts due him, submitted to the Lord Treasurer, included:

By pearls for her Majesty	£1300
By Lady Leicester	2500
By Earl of Derby	1200
For Sir Francis Drake when he went around the world	2000
For Sir Francis when he went to Carthegena	16600

A stupendous sum in those days.

To say that John Martin is typical of his associates in the Virginia adventure in every respect may be inaccurate, but they had common experiences and they possessed common qualities, dauntless patriotism, restless energy, and religious zeal. They were all great individuals, sons of the English Renaissance—products of the English counties, of the London of the great merchants, Thomas Smith and the Sandys; of those mighty sons of Neptune, Drake, Howard, Raleigh, and Grenville; of the soldier courtiers, the Earls of Leicester and Essex; of the poets and philosophers, Shakespeare, Johnson, and Bacon; and of the great press agent of adventure who recorded their deeds, Richard Hakluyt, the minister. London was a city about the size of present day Richmond, Virginia. These men and their friends were necessarily acquaintances or even intimates if their aspirations and high strung dispositions permitted. They met in their gentlemen's clubs—the Mermaid and the Miter Taverns—at their homes, and in court. The patron of Shakespeare was Southampton; Hakluyt dedicated his voyages to Sir Walter Raleigh. William Strachey's letter to a noble lady must have been read by her or her husband to Shakespeare, else *The Tempest* would scarcely have been written; Sir Francis Bacon, the nephew of Elizabeth's great prime minister probably helped draw the second charter of the Virginia Company. The point is that the background and atmosphere of the Virginia enterprise were essentially and broadly Elizabethan, that these Englishmen with calculated deliberation set the stage for the greatest of dramas, the birth of a new nation.

On April 26, 1607, by the old-style calendar, the *Susan Constant,* the *Godspeed* and the *Discovery* sailed into the Chesapeake Bay, and a land of such goodly tall trees and fresh springs greeted them that the company was almost ravished at the sight.

On the *Susan Constant* a sealed box containing articles of instruction was opened. Captains Newport, Gosnold, and Ratcliffe together with Edward Maria Wingfield, John Smith, John Martin, and George Kendall were named to His Majesty's Council for his first colony in Virginia. The King's government at home ordained that the Council "shall by majority part choose one of the same not being a minister of God's word to be president." The Council of Captains, who were certainly not ministers of God's word and who had little in common other than their love for adventure, their vaulting ambition, and their distrust for each other, were admonished in the first instructions to their government concerning the separation of the church and state and so they elected Wingfield, a Roman Catholic, their first president.

With their government organized they sailed up Powhatan's great river and selected for their permanent settlement a low lying peninsula which had little to commend it. They had a serious fight with the Indians in which five members of the Council, including Martin, were wounded; how seriously is not related. Martin as Master of the Ordnance was directed to proceed forthwith to the erection of Fort James. This he did with great dispatch. The triangular structure 420 by 300 by 300 feet was completed on June 20, the day before Captain Newport sailed for England. That the fort saved the colony from extinction cannot be doubted, for by January, of the 104 persons left at the settlement, only 38 survived. Summer sickness and Indian attacks had taken a ghastly toll. Martin's only son was among the dead. The survivors were emaciated. Distrust was rampant, food and supplies were exhausted. "Their drink was water, their houses castles in the air." Ratcliffe, Smith, and Martin combined to depose Wingfield as president, choosing Ratcliffe in his place. Martin charged that Wingfield did "slack the service in the Collonye, and . . . hath starved my sonne and denyed him a spoonful of beere."

The new president, Ratcliffe, struck a blacksmith who returned the blow and for this insubordination was condemned to be hanged. The offender saved himself by giving evidence against Kendall for conspiring desertion. The trio then condemned Kendall to be shot, but he protested being sentenced by Ratcliffe because his name was Sicklemore not Ratcliffe. Martin solved the problem by himself pronouncing judgment and seeing to the execution. At this time Smith described Martin as respectable in character, "verie honest, and wishing the best good, yet so sicke and weake."

Trading with the Indians and supplying the colony with native food appears to have been largely the responsibility of Smith and Martin. Every expedition was fraught with the gravest hazards. Courage unlimited, complete self-control, and a heart incapable of the sense of fear were requisite qualities. By the effort of these men the colony was fed.

On a foraging trip in December, Smith was captured by Indians and taken to Powhatan. He saved his life by amusing his captors with some toys and a compass. In his *True Relation* Smith says that he was treated kindly by the great chief and sent to Jamestown under escort. It was nineteen years later that he recounted the Pocahontas incident which has become a part of Virginia history. During Smith's absence and because he had been reported dead, Ratcliffe, by virtue of his two votes as president against Martin's one, swore in Archer as a member of the Council. Smith wrote this account of his return:

"Each man with the truest signes of joy they could express welcomed me, except *Maister Archer*, . . . who was then in my absence, sworne Counsellour, though not with the consent of Captaine *Martin*:

"Great blame and imputation was laide upon mee by them [Archer, &c.], for the losse of our two men which the *Indians* slew: insomuch that they purposed to depose me. But in the midst of my miseries, it pleased God to send *Captain Nuport*: who arriving there the same night [8 *Jan. 1608*], so tripled our joy as for a while these plots against me were deferred. . . . Now was Maister [Matthew] *Scrivener*, captaine *Martin*, and my selfe, called Counsellers [*i.e., to the exclusion of Archer*]."

When Newport arrived on January 8, bringing with him supplies and more immigrants, he found only 38 survivors of the 104 settlers he had left at Jamestown the previous June. The new supply gave new life, and peace and order prevailed until he left in April, taking Wingfield and Archer with him to answer in London for their misdemeanors. Now Martin and Ratcliffe were in virtual control of the colony. They did, however, grant some slight authority to Smith and Scrivener.

On June 2 Martin returned to England and took John Smith's *True Relation* with him. He must have been a very busy man in London. About this time his daughter Dorcas married Captain George Bargrave, and the affairs of the Company required his activities and interests. He assisted in organizing the second supply and recruiting seventy useful immigrants, most of whom were skilled laborers and artisans. Broadsides were distributed calling on all workers who wished to go to Virginia to come to Sir Thomas Smith's house in Philpot Lane. Opportunities in Virginia for the thrifty and industrious were extolled widely from the pulpit and many from all classes volunteered. Martin with the aid of Smith's *True Relation* succeeded admirably.

In addition to materials and workers, the colonists needed a practical and workable charter. They needed free enterprise and the right to govern themselves. Above all they needed the right of free men to enjoy the fruits of their labor. Their arguments and presentations were effective. All they sought was granted by the King. The first American businessmen had the chance to go into business. Sir Thomas Smith and the Sandys, perhaps with the help of Sir Francis Bacon, drew the great Second Charter, a milestone marking the beginning, the primitive of the American system of government. Martin was named a permanent member of the Council.

In the spring, a fleet consisting of nine ships with 500 passengers aboard, under the command of Admiral Sir George Somers in the *Sea Venture*, and including Captain Martin commanding the *Falcon*, sailed for Virginia.

The accounts of the hurricane which scattered the fleet and wrecked the *Sea Venture* with the Admiral and Governor on the "still vexed Bermuthes," the death of John Rolfe's child named Bermuda, and the construction of two pinnaces out of native cedar are well-known and are integral parts of the Virginia story. It suffices to say, Martin brought the *Falcon* and his wards safely to Jamestown.

Upon arrival, Martin began replacement of buildings by more serviceable structures, for among his artisans were carpenters and some skilled in the manufacture of brick and tile. There were attempts at industry and dreams of profitable business. Briefly an air of confidence developed. The first English wedding in America had taken place. John Laydon, a carpenter, married Ann Burras, Mrs. Forrest's servant, and to this day the descendants of this homely union of modest industry and labor probably survive in Virginia.

Smith, the only member of the Council remaining, would admit no associates, and Somers, with the commissions for the new council, was shipwrecked. Archer wrote, "Now did we all lament the absence of our Governour, for the contentions began to grow, . . . inasmuch as the President [Captain Smith], to strengthen his authority, accorded with the Mariners, and gave not any due respect to many worthy Gentleman."

The worthy gentleman, being thus disturbed, with Archer's assistance combined against Smith and chose Francis West, Lord Delaware's brother, as governor. Archer continued, "This choice of him they made not to disturbe the old President during his time, . . . (but he had already during this month of August once given up the Presidency to Captain Martin, who resigned it back to him again)."

The discord in the Council came to a head early in October. Smith had sent Captain Francis West to the falls of the James with one hundred men, who were ambushed and treated roughly by the Indians. Belatedly Smith came to their rescue and there arose a great division between them. West accused Smith of betraying him, so Smith ran off with all the ammunition. He was careless with the powder he had on his person which exploded and burned him so painfully that he jumped into the river and almost drowned. Smith, as a matter of course, told stories of his own heroism and suffering, but the facts are that upon his arrival at Jamestown he was deposed by Martin, Archer, and Ratcliffe and sent to England under charges "with 30 unruly youths, none of whom were desired at Jamestown." "Smithe beinge an Ambityous unworthy and vayneglorious fellowe attempt-inge to take all Mens Authoreties from them . . . aymeinge att A Soveraigne Rule withoutt the Assistance of the cowncell was iustely depryved of all," and George Percy, against his earnest protest, was elected president *pro tempore*.

The winter of 1609-1610, known as the starving time, was one of unbelievable tragedy. The Indians waged a ruthless war of extermi-nation against the colony. Dissension, disease, and despair exacted a tremendous penalty. Good laborers and artificers deserted to Powhatan and lived a brief idyllic life in their sylvan harem. Life existed by a slender thread. The very skins of their horses were prepared by baking and stewing into dainty welcome food. It was reported that, "So great was our famine, that a Salvage we slew and buried, the poorer sort tooke him up again and eat him; and so did divers one another boyled and stewed with roots and herbs: And one amongst the rest did kill his wife, powdered [salted] her, and had eaten part of her before it was knowne." Of the five hundred persons in the colony in October, six months later there remained not above sixty.

This calamitous state did Sir Thomas Gates, the governor, and Sir George Somers find when they arrived May 24 with the Charter and survivors of the wrecked *Sea Venture*. Life was desperate for those who had come to find new homes. The end of human endurance had been reached. They voted to abandon Jamestown, to return to Eng-land, all but one— "save only John Martin." The will of this slight man had never been conquered, the goodly land still held him en-thralled. Perhaps it was because his only son, "the hope of his old age," lay in one of the unmarked graves. Perhaps it was a vision and a steel nerve; but most certainly his blood was mingled forever with Virginia soil.

To wipe out the last vestige of their sufferings, in a spirit of venge-fulness, some of the colonists wished to burn the fort. John Martin certainly sided with Gates, the governor, who prevented them from doing so. With their ordnance the colonists fired a final salute to their dead and drifted down the river with the tide. The tide turned, and they met abundant relief—Lord Delaware with food, clothing, and supplies, with good physicians and worthy divines, with thrifty la-borers and skilled artisans. The English settlement in Virginia was permanent. The course was clear and the first chapter in the birth of a great nation came to an end.

With the arrival of Lord Delaware a period of substantial development began, a period of profit for the industrious, of growing evidence of success and a realization of some of the opportunities which had led immigrants to Virginia by the hundreds. Delaware left Martin off the Council in the new government. Thomas Dale, the deputy governor, who succeeded in 1611, appointed Martin to positions of trust, but not until 1624 was Martin again on the Council. It was an authoritative government which functioned, and the disastrous dissensions ceased. The plantations grew and prospered. Brick took the place of clapboard, tile took the place of thatch, streets were laid out, a landing wharf was built, and traders plied the rivers.

The governor sent the intrepid Captain Argall to trade on the rivers to the north. He found and rescued Henry Spelman, an English boy who had been left with Powhatan two years earlier by John Smith. Spelman's account of Smith's attention to the Indian reflects little credit on Smith and reveals some of the ruthlessness and vainglory in Smith's character. On this trip Argall acquired some Indian friends who a few years later were principals in his most famous business transaction—the purchase of the Princess Pocahontas for a copper kettle.

The possession of Pocahontas at Jamestown brought peace. The practical Dale and the practical Councilors readily acquiesced, if indeed they did not encourage, her marriage to the recently bereaved John Rolfe. In any event, the planning was good.

It is a pity that so few of Martin's letters have been found and that he did not write a True Relation. The apparent fact is that he was too busy with critical problems of survival and so his paths must be followed by evidence from other sources. What a story he could have told! This slight man, fighter, builder, councilor, sufferer from many wounds, bereaved father, at the time of Lord Delaware's arrival was one of sixty survivors of more than a thousand colonists who had come to Virginia. There is no evidence of his ever having been discouraged —of ever slackening his effort. Each new hope brought to him a new opportunity and increased his activity. He engaged in everything which affected the colony. With peace his competition and aggressiveness in trade along the rivers became a vexatious problem. In agriculture he tried everything he could lay his hand on. He promoted the silk industry and was experimenting with tobacco seed from Trinidad before John Rolfe's arrival. Ralph Hamor, Secretary of the Council, visited his plantation in 1614 and wrote that he had seen "even of the naturall, and wilde plants, which Captaine *Martin*, who much delighteth in those businesses, hath made, exceeding fine and strong silke." Hamor might have added: "All the variety of needful fruit and vegetables thrive and prosper well of which husbandry and thrift we have made many experiments. There have been brought here plants from the West Indies, vines from France, tobacco from Trinidad."

As deputy governor, Thomas Dale had arrived in May 1611 with three ships, 300 immigrants, implements, and supplies. In August Governor Gates arrived with 300 men, with cattle and hogs and all manner of munitions. He dispatched Dale up the river to build the city of Henrico. This settlement on Farrar's Island was to be the metropolis of the river plantations. Its streets were wide, its buildings were of brick, and it contained the first formal hospital in America, which contained space for eighty patients.

A University of Henrico was proposed to which subscriptions were received, including 10,000 acres of land from the Company. All inhabitants and the community were obliterated in the massacre of 1622.

Apparently Martin had no part in the building of Henrico. He was occupied with his growing flocks and herds, with the servants he had brought from England, and with schemes for the future. He undoubtedly had his eye on another peninsula in the river some twelve miles above Jamestown if, in fact, he was not already clearing away its trees and cultivating its lands. In the winter of 1615-1616 he and Rolfe loaded the good ship *Treasurer* with a full cargo of "exceeding *good* tobacco, sasfrix, pych, potashes, sturoyon & cavyare." In the spring they sailed away for the markets of London taking with them Sir Thomas Dale, Pocahontas, and young Master Rolfe. In Martin's especial care was the Spanish spy Molena who had been taken at Point Comfort some three years before.

In England the influence of the Martins had certainly not waned. Sir Julius Caesar was on the Privy Council. Sir Richard was esteemed as a banker, a statesman, and a public servant. John Martin's daughter Dorcas, named after his mother and his sister, had married Captain George Bargrave. Martin, like the Roman centurion, was a man having authority.

Martin got from the London powers the peninsula he yearned for, as well as rights and privileges unique in American annals. The patent was signed by Pembroke, Southampton, Thomas Smith, Julius Caesar, Francis Bacon, and others and granted immunity to Martin, his heirs and assigns, from any obligation to obey the laws of the colony "save only to defend it against its foreign and domestical enemies." It created a distinct and separate estate—a feudal principality in a rapidly growing democratic community. The provisions of this patent were a cause of great criticism and much dissatisfaction in the colony. Martin, in defending it before the Council, the House of Burgesses, and the Virginia Company, claimed that he had earned every privilege and every acre he had received, and asserted he would defend them against all comers. To honor his wife he gave her family name Brandon to the 5,000 acre grant. He was riding his high tide of success and ready to exploit the fruits of his labors. He entered into a trading partnership with his son-in-law's brother, Captain John Bargrave.

Rolfe wrote, "Every man [in Virginia is] sitting under his fig tree in safety, gathering and reaping the fruites of their labors with much ioy and comfort," and "The *Farmors* live at most ease, yet by their good indeavors bring yerely much plenty to the Plantation."

When prosperity came to the colony Martin was over fifty years old, and as he grew older he grew more exacting of his associates and more sensitive to attacks on what he conceived to be his rights. He seems to have been opposed to almost every other proprietor. He refused to cooperate with the Council, to conform to its edicts or to pay its taxes. From his return to Virginia in the summer of 1616, to the end of his life, he was embroiled in controversies. The planters and the Council resented the special treatment accorded him and complained to the London Company of the "ill effects which have followed those his exorbitant priviledges, namely that hereupon Captain Martin hath refused to submitt himselfe to the lawes." He was excluded from the Council. In 1619 when the first House of Burgesses met, his two elected burgesses from Brandon were refused their seats because this first American parliament decided the possessors of special privileges and immunities could have no voice in governing free citizens. The partnership with John Bargrave had been anything but successful and litigation piled up. His patent was attacked in England and thither he went to defend it. At this time the colony consisted of six hundred people, "about three hundred Head of Cattle, some Goats, and infinite Numbers of Hogs."

In twelve years the Company had expended £80,000 and had little to show for it. The adventurers had received nothing for this capital except the land grants they had received in Virginia. Discontent within developed, and the liberal Sir Edwin Sandys succeeded the conservative Sir Thomas Smith, merchant prince of Philpot Lane. The controversy over Martin's patent became a major issue. In the Company's Court for February 1622 the patent was voided as having been illegally granted and Martin was offered "a newe Patent upon surrender of his old, with as large and ample privileges as they may or can graunt by his Majesty's Letters Patente." Finally, Martin surrendered for the first and last time in his life. He accepted a new grant. It was sufficient without the extra territorial privileges. He submitted suggestions to the Privy Council for making Virginia a Royal Colony, and in this he had Sir Julius Caesar's aid and counsel and possibly Captain Samuel Argall's. Then he returned to Virginia and to his Brandon. Discord and mismanagement had numbered the days of his Company, but it had done its work and served a great purpose. In 1624 the King recalled the Charter and Virginia became a Royal Colony.

In 1626, John Martin, then in London, petitioned his most excellent Majesty Charles I, asking protection to go about and settle all of his debts, which he was both willing and able to do, and in particular he asked protection from his erstwhile partner, Captain John Bargrave. He recites that on his land "he built a Towne, cleared much ground, bredd many cattell and tame Hoges. . . . gathered a computent quantitie of goods . . . for payinge of his debts, and the relievinge of himself, his wife, and children; they were unjustly detayned by one Mr. *John Bargrave,* in whom he had reposed great confidence. . . . [He was] forced to come for England. . . . where he hath been in suit this two yeares. . . . Since which time all your supplicants houses in Virginia are burnt, his goods, stock, and rents all loste amountinge to the balence of £2000."

He must have settled his accounts very promptly for before the end of the year he was back in Virginia writing letters of advice about colonial affairs to his very loving brother, Sir Julius Caesar. Under the Royal Government he must have prospered. He died about 1632, the last survivor of the ancient adventurers, and his body probably occupies an unknown grave on the land he conquered by the river he loved. His grandson, Robert Bargrave, inherited his land which he sold in 1635 to Richard Quiney of Stratford on Avon, the son and namesake of the "loving friend and fellow countryman of Mr. William Shakespeare," and brother of Thomas Quiney who married the daughter of the poet.

VI.

POCAHONTAS' PLAYMATES

T RADITIONAL evidence has painted a pretty picture of a little princess of Virginia's primeval forests playing on the streets of Jamestown with the children of the settlers, teaching them the calls of the wild things, the use of the bow, and turning handsprings simply for the joy of living. Perhaps historians have done the reputation of Pocahontas violence by attributing to her heroics for which the artless Indian maid could hardly have been responsible and which really added little or nothing to her stature as a courageous and remarkable woman. The purpose here, however, is not to dwell on Pocahontas but rather to call attention to three other little girls of her same age who, in the Fort and on the Island, must have sometimes been her companions. It is interesting that the four little girls have had descendants living in Virginia and sharing Virginia's fortunes from the founding of Jamestown to this date. It is interesting that the three little white girls lie buried in Pocahontas' native land and Pocahontas lies at Gravesend in an English churchyard.

Ann Burras, age thirteen, arrived in Jamestown in 1608 aboard the *Mary and Margaret* as maid to Mrs. Forrest, wife of Thomas Forrest, Gentleman. The little ship carried a distinguished company including two members of the Council, Francis West, the brother of Lord De La Warr, besides fourteen tradesmen, twelve laborers, and some Dutchmen. Neither the names of Mrs. Forrest nor that of her husband appear again in the available records, but the child, Ann Burras, married John Laydon, a carpenter, who had come over on the *Susan Constant* in the spring of 1607. This was the first marriage of English

41

in America. In due course it was blessed with the arrival of a little girl whom the parents named Virginia.

What an American story there must be in that of the Laydons! The record of their particular deeds and adventures is lost. They lived through all the tribulations of the early years—epidemics, starvation, and massacres. They conquered the wilderness about them, and they prospered. Their four daughters, Virginia, Katherine, Alice, and Margaret, are listed in the census of 1625, and in 1636 John and Ann, as ancient planters, were granted ". . . an additional 1250 acres in Warwick River County." It is probable that John survived all the original company who came to Jamestown in 1607.

Whatever privileges the Laydons enjoyed as ancient adventurers they most certainly earned. The chroniclers of their times did not record the modest part John took in building and defending the Fort and the Church in which the minister Robert Hunt married him and Ann and which he must have attended faithfully. Doubtless, as a laborer, he had no voice in the decision to abandon the Colony when only John Martin is recorded as voting "nay". But he and Ann turned again up the great River with Lord De La Warr and never in their lives left Virginia. The historians of that era did not record Ann's services to the sick and dying during the starving time nor the heroism of a teenage girl in the raw and tragic wilderness, but they did recite punishment meted out to her for a breach of discipline, probably in 1611.

Under the regime of Sir Thomas Dale, Ann Laydon, Jane Wright, and other women were assigned the task of making shirts for the colonists. If they exceeded their allotment of material they lost their allowance of food. Other deficiencies incurred various punishments. The record reads: "Because their thread was naught and would not serve, they took out a ravel in the lower part of the shirt to make an end of the work, so the shirts of those that had raveled out part proved shorter than the rest, for which fact Ann Laydon and Jane Wright were whipped, and Ann being with child miscarried."

At the other end of the English social ladder there was another young lady, another girl of thirteen years who had felt the strong appeal of the New World of opportunity. Her name was Temperance Flowerdieu. Tradition has it that even then she was susceptible to the charm of a young soldier, possibly a cousin, whose name was George

Yeardley. Their dreams too are not recorded, but there remains abundant evidence of their courage.

They left England in the spring of 1609 in a convoy of nine ships with 500 passengers, all under the command of Sir George Somers. Temperance was on the *Falcon*, the Vice-Admiral of the fleet, and George was on the *Sea Venture*, the Admiral. "A most terrible hurricane struck the fleet and scattered it." The *Sea Venture* was wrecked on Bermuda, two of the ships were never heard of again, but John Martin, the ancient adventurer, who had also sailed around the world with Drake, brought the *Falcon*, the *Blessing*, the *Lion*, and the *Unity* to Jamestown. Yeardley, John Rolfe and his first wife, Newport, and other survivors reached Jamestown almost a year later on the *Deliverance* and the *Patience*, little ships that had been built from the wreckage of the *Sea Venture* and Bermuda cedars. Strachey, who wrote the letter to the "Noble Lady", which was the inspiration of Shakespeare's *The Tempest*, was on the *Deliverance*. Could it be that Ferdinand and Miranda were counterparts of Temperance Flowerdieu and George Yeardley? They were the same age.

This was in 1610. Temperance was fourteen years old. Other women were in the Colony. John Smith had been sent home as George Percy wrote, "with other unruly youths, none of whom were desired." John Rolfe's wife died. Life was confronted by harsh realities. Men and women survived through their fortitude and faith in their destiny. If anyone knew the Pocahontas-Smith legend nothing was said or written about it, then or later. However, there is a record of an intriguing ballet which the Indian princess and her maidens, as naked as Diana, performed midst autumn leaves for the entertainment of Newport, Smith, and other dignitaries while the great chief laid before them the finest foods the forests and rivers could yield.

There is no adequate record of those who lived and those who died and lie in the unmarked graves around the cross erected in 1957. How long Temperance stayed in Jamestown and how many trips across the great ocean were made by George is not recorded. However, in 1618, they were married in London. George was knighted by King James and sailed with his lady on his honeymoon to Virginia, commissioned as Royal Governor. Their flesh and blood and that of their descendants is forever a part of Virginia.

It was Sir George Yeardley who brought the Great Charter to Virginia and called the first free election in the New World for legislative representatives. He encouraged his relatives and those of Temperance to come to Virginia. Their names appear in the land records and on the honor rolls of the Colony.

The Yeardleys set high standards of public service and community responsibility which, at a later date, became characteristic of the plantation aristocracy. Sir George died in 1627 and lies buried in the Church at Jamestown. He was survived by Temperance, two sons, Argall and Francis, and a daughter Elizabeth. The communion service of Southampton Hundred entrusted to his care is now at Saint John's Church, Hampton, Virginia. His will provided liberal bequests to the charities of the day, and the remainder of his estate he divided among his family.

In those days women did not long remain unmarried; so, in some haste Temperance deeded all the property she had inherited from Sir George to their children and married, probably the most prominent man in the Colony, the brother of Lord De La Warr, Francis West, who succeeded Yeardley as governor.

There were many women at Jamestown in those days who had fitted into England's stratified social structure somewhere between Ann Burras and Temperance Flowerdieu. Nothing is known of Ann's antecedents. Of Temperance's much is known. She was of the gentry of Norfolk County. Her mother was the daughter and heiress of John Stanley. Her paternal grandparents were related to Robert Dudley, Earl of Leicester. Her family connections were prominent and their position firmly established.

The little Indian princess must have had other playmates on the streets of Jamestown. Sisley Jordan came over on the *Swan* in 1610. She was then nine years old, and so far as is known she never left Virginia. She is listed in the muster of 1625 as twenty-four years old, a widow living with her three children on her deceased husband's plantation known as Jordan's Journey, Charles City Corporation. The plantation was overrun by Indians during the Massacre of 1622. What deeds of heroism were performed by Sisley in defense of her little family are not known. Her husband, who had also come to Virginia in 1610, had been a member of the first House of Burgesses and was a member of the committee to review the first four books of the Great Charter.

Sisley must have been fair to behold, in addition to being an heiress, for two days after Samuel Jordan died Greville Pooley, minister of the Established Church, ardently sought her hand in matrimony. Sisley succumbed to his entreaties but insisted that the ceremonies be delayed until after the arrival of her unborn Jordan baby. This concession to propriety cost Pooley his bride. In the meantime William Farrar, who had qualified as administrator of Samuel Jordan's estate, apparently felt that he could the better perform his fiduciary duties by moving into the Jordan household, for the muster records reveal that Sisley Jordan and William Farrar "maintained a joint household." This romantic arrangement culminated in their marriage, but not before the discarded lover, Mr. Pooley, had instituted breach of promise proceedings in the General Court seeking specific performance. The contest was referred to the Council of the Virginia Company in London who tactfully returned the suit to Jamestown with the notation that they ". . . knew not how to decide so nice a difference."

In the first ten years of the Colony there were all told several hundred women at Jamestown. There were the three daughters of Sir Thomas Gates: Margaret, Mary, and Elizabeth, whose mother had died on the voyage over. There were the young, sometimes beautiful, wives of adventurous young men from every walk of English life, and there were the indentured servants.

Ann Burras, Temperance Flowerdieu and Sisley Jordan can represent all the unsung heroines of that heroic age. They possessed that courage, stamina, and faith in the new land characteristic of all their "sisters." They embodied the spirit and fortitude of all the silent partners of the master adventurers in the New World, who founded a nation and whose blood is the strength and the backbone of America today. Ann, Temperance, and Sisley can represent all of them. They were contemporaries of Pocahontas but, unlike Pocahontas, their bodies are forever a part of Virginia's soil.

VII.

WILLIAM RANDOLPH

I N the 175 years of Virginia's colonial existence the Lower Peninsula was one of the greatest and most productive political and social laboratories of all time. Here, in an atmosphere laden with new concepts of human dignity and human rights, practical men and women sought solutions to life's pressing problems. In the course of their labors they raised the curtain on expanding ethical horizons and evolved principles which govern the nation's cohesive society and make the United States the mightiest of nations. The leaders of that seventeenth century society were essentially businessmen who took calculated risks that their labor and their capital might yield profits. By and large, they were of the great English middle class—merchants, shipowners, small manufacturers, skilled artisans—not reckless adventurers primarily seeking excitement and plunder from wealth garnered by primitive peoples. Those Englishmen were home builders who sought and found independence in the cultivation of the soil and the exploitation of the natural wealth of the forest. Raleigh's lieutenant Sir Richard Grenville had indicated the course by describing "the soil as the goodliest under the cope of Heaven." The prospect of hard labor did not entice the slothful nor did the dangers of the raw wilderness lure the timid.

The three charters granted by James I of England between 1606 and 1618 to that famous association of adventurers known as the London Company furnished the foundation. The corporate organization, and rules for the conduct of business, which they devised, supplied a plan for establishing and developing a government responsive to its citizens and a society conscious of its obligations to the commonweal. The importance of those charters to the Western World can hardly be overemphasized. Primarily, they recognized the dignity of productive labor and the right of every man to earn the honorable respect of his fellows. The quarterly courts of the shareholders of the Company furnished a diagram for the creation of a government resting on the consent of the governed, the Virginia House of Burgesses, the first representative legislative assembly in America.

Progenitors of the great families—Carter, Randolph, Byrd, Page, Nelson, and Fitzhugh—understood the exactions the New World demanded and the rewards it offered. They came, acquired land, and went to work. These and their progeny were the technicians in the great tidewater Virginia laboratory.

The story of our colonial development and the crystallization of the fundamental principles of our government, those embodied in the Constitution of the United States, may well be related by means of the biographies of outstanding men of one great family. The family founded by William Randolph of Turkey Island, which included among its sons and grandsons Sir John Randolph, Peyton Randolph, Edmund Randolph, Randolph of Roanoke, Jefferson, Marshall and many others, has played a critical part in the nation's history.

It is interesting to look into the English background of this family concerning which little was known until recent research furnished some clues, and also to review some of the activities of the founder of the Virginia family. Perhaps the political upheavals in England and the ensuing social unrest caused the early Virginians to neglect or ignore their ties with the old country. Perhaps the new society which dignified productive labor and recognized creative ability caused them to depreciate the efficacy of tradition and inherited privileges. In any event, William Randolph, like the Carters, the Lees, the Byrds, the Washingtons, and their contemporaries, left little information to help the genealogist to trace their lineages. The civil wars had been grievously expensive to the great English middle class and the restored monarchy with its dissolute court did not inspire confidence. The Virginians had tasted a degree of independence and they liked it. In theory, they were Royalists, but throughout their colonial existence they challenged royal authority. Their pattern of home and life was that of the English gentry, but pride in ancestry was not one of their conceits.

After Cromwell's battles of Preston, Dunbar, and Worcester, great numbers of prisoners fell into the hands of the parliamentary forces. A committee created for the purpose was authorized to dispose to the colonies all prisoners under the rank of field officer. This, the finest kind of human material for America, lacked neither enterprise nor courage.

The name Randolph, with its variations in spelling, appears with more or less regularity in English and Scottish records from the time of William the Conqueror. Men of the name were ministers, knights, diplomats, poets—always politicians and frequently prominent. Their history was part of England's history. Thomas, the first Earl of Moray, had played a critical part in the battle of Bannockburn. Thomas, of a later date, was an ambassador of Queen Elizabeth and as such, amid mingled shadows of light and darkness, acted his part in the international intrigues of the era. He was deeply involved in the conspiracies against Mary, Queen of the Scots. Another Thomas, the granduncle of William of Turkey Island, was poet laureate in the reign of James I. The names John, Thomas, William, and Robert appear in every generation in varying degrees of national importance. A penchant for public service and the similarity of the arms of the families, supply the genealogist with important clues to relationships. William's great grandfather, Robert, spelled his name Randall until his wife, Rose Roberts, insisted that he spell the family name Randolph in order more properly to identify themselves. This Robert and Rose had a son, William, so wild and wayward that the father disinherited the son and left him "only one goat." Upon receipt of this legacy, William nailed his inheritance to the door of his father's house and departed to seek his fortune. He readily found profitable employment and married Elizabeth Lane, the widow of Thomas West of Lord Delaware's family. Their son, Richard, married Elizabeth Ryland and they were the parents of the founder of the Virginia family.

William Randolph landed in Jamestown in 1672. Figuratively speaking, or perhaps actually, he hung out his business shingle "Wm. Randolph, Undertaker," which signified that he was a general contractor and would undertake almost anything for a profit. His capital was chiefly the endowment of a superb body, an alert mind, and boundless energy. He was twenty-one years old. The parish register of Morton Morrell contains a record of his baptism on November 7, 1650. Specifically why he came to Jamestown is not known, but his

Uncle Henry had lived there since 1635. He had recently lost a son whose name was William. Family loyalty and family pride were ever characteristic of the Randolphs, so perhaps the uncle sent for the nephew to exploit the opportunities of the New World and build on the foundation he had established. Among the colonists, Henry was a man of achievement and dignity. He had acquired a river plantation, served as a clerk in the House of Burgesses and at the time of William's arrival, he was living in the old State House at Jamestown, which he had purchased and converted into his residence. It is thought that William lived in this house until his uncle's death, which occurred a little over a year after William's arrival.

The young man made the most of his opportunities in the New World. He grew in favor with men of influence and particularly in the good graces of Sir William and Lady Berkeley. So, on the death of his uncle, William succeeded him to the position of clerk in the Assembly. Two years after his arrival in Virginia he was granted 591 acres of land at the junction of Swift Creek and the Appomattox River "for transporting twelve persons to the colony." This land was adjacent to that of Henry Isham, his future father-in-law, who had come to Virginia in 1656. About this same time William Randolph was given 10,000 pounds of tobacco for his services to the Assembly. The very personable young man was taking his place among America's first businessmen. He built a house on the Appomatox land and according to contemporary records it was well stocked with the essential goods and chattels of the period. In 1675 he married Mary Isham.

The Ishams had a lineage as long as the Randolphs. They never soared to heights of great prominence but they were always of the gentry and had occupied positions of dignity and honor in England for centuries. The forebears of Henry had lived at Pitchley, the family manor in Northamptonshire, since the thirteenth century and their records in the most complete form are preserved to this day.

The alacrity with which William gained a position of importance in the colony was not due to the vibrant prosperity of its people. A shortsighted English Parliament had passed the Navigation Act excluding the Dutch and French traders from the rivers. Tobacco was selling at distressed prices, and the English merchants, taking advantage of their monopoly, were demanding exorbitant prices for essentials which the planters had to have to build their homes, cultivate their land, and protect themselves from the Indians. Governor Berkeley encouraged the monopolies and took advantage of them himself. Through his acts and the distribution of land, a few powerful landowners were vastly enriched at the expense of the small farmers. The few Cavaliers who had come to Virginia were patronized. Virginia was heading slowly but inexorably towards a social order composed of landed proprietors and serfs. In 1671, the aging Royal Governor, at the age of sixty-four, had married Frances, thirty-six, the daughter of Lord Culpeper. It was natural that Sir William and his fair lady, beaming in the reflected glory of the Restoration, vengeful for the fancied outrages committed by the Cromwellians, exercised their royal prerogatives and fostered a regal atmosphere in their capital. It was natural that they took an interest in the handsome, young Randolph.

Historians have attempted to analyze the causes of the metamorphoses in the character of Sir William Berkeley. They have generally abandoned the attempt in a summary comparison to Dr. Jekyll and Mr. Hyde. It is true that from his arrival in Virginia as Royal Governor in 1642 until he was replaced during the period of the Commonwealth, he was a benevolent, constructive ruler of an industrious, determined people. The role he assumed as defender of the small farmer and advocate of liberal reforms in government endeared him to all. He built his residence, the first great house in Virginia, at Green Spring, and on that plantation of 5,000 acres he maintained an operation in agronomy which was, in fact, an agricultural experimental station conducted for the benefit of the Colony.

At this time there was no caste system in Virginia. Opportunity to acquire property and positions of honor invited the honest and industrious. Former indentured servants took their places in an emerging aristocracy of successful planters. Governor Berkeley was the hero of this homogenous society. A grateful people assumed and paid his royal pensions during the English civil wars. It was quite natural that when Governor Matthews became disgusted with the course of affairs in England after the Restoration and resigned, that the Assembly elected Berkeley to the office. It was also quite natural that those who constituted the very backbone of the Colony were slow to realize the change in Sir William's character and to recognize in their former hero an arch enemy. First they petitioned, then they threatened. The hundreds of small farmers, the yeomen, who had won their freedom by hard labor, were ready to defend their rights with their lives.

While the people in Virginia were slowly approaching crossroads of destiny, another young man, three years William Randolph's senior, was finishing his formal education at Cambridge and Gray's Inn. It is interesting that Nathaniel Bacon's background was fundamentally the same as that of Berkeley and Randolph. He was the son of the wealthy owner of Friston Hall and the great nephew of the eminent Sir Francis. He was educated at Cambridge and studied law at Gray's Inn. Fortunately for the Western World and unfortunately for the Bacons, he fell in love with Elizabeth, the high-spirited daughter of Sir Edward Duke. Why Sir Edward opposed the marriage is not known, but oppose he did, and so violently that he disinherited his determined daughter. The marriage, however, was one of true love and greatest devotion. This event, together with an unfortunate business transaction, caused Nathaniel's father to think that it might be wise for his son to seek his fortune in Virginia. So, with a stake of £1800 cash, Nathaniel and his family boarded a tobacco ship and set out for the New World. This, very briefly, is the background of the man whom a contemporary historian has denominated the "torchbearer of the American Revolution."

It is dangerous to use superlatives and it is difficult to analyze events with acceptable precisions. Yet, it is certain that Berkeley and Bacon represented violently opposing ideologies and interests in a critical period in the development of the Colony. For the creation of our way of life, the defeat of both at that time was probably necessary. Randolph's career, so to speak, was the resultant of the opposing forces of that conflict. He was a beneficiary of the departure of both. He was opposed to Bacon; his father-in-law was opposed to Berkeley. He suffered financially during the so-called Rebellion, but by one means or another he acquired Bacon's estate at Curles on the James after it had been confiscated by the government.

Randolph maintained the even tenor of his ways, walked with the great, and nurtured a sympathetic contact with the earnest yeomanry. He scrupulously met his obligations of service to the Colony as Justice, as Burgess, as an officer of the militia, as a member of the Council. He acquired land and prospered. He educated his children according to standards of the day, and after the fashion of the English gentry, he trained his sons for useful public service and in the thrifty management of competent estates. In contemporary letters and official records, he is found an agreeable associate in business and a welcome companion in social intercourse with William Byrd, Francis Epps, Richard Cocke, the Ludwells, the Armisteads, and the Beverleys. His sons married their daughters and their sons married his daughters. Old county documents indicate a useful and constructive association in business between William Randolph and Thomas Jefferson—two great-grandfathers of the author of the Declaration of Independence.